WELCOME

FOR SOME FUN

SOCCER HISTORY.

BY KICK BOOKS PUBLISHING

THIS BOOK IS A WORK OF NONFICTION, CREATED FOR EDUCATIONAL AND ENTERTAINMENT PURPOSES. WHILE EVERY EFFORT HAS BEEN MADE TO ENSURE ACCURACY, SOME DETAILS MAY BE SUBJECT TO CHANGE OVER TIME.

ALL RIGHTS RESERVED. NO PART OF THIS BOOK MAY BE COPIED, STORED, OR SHARED IN ANY FORM WITHOUT WRITTEN PERMISSION FROM THE PUBLISHER,

FIRST EDITION
KICK BOOKS PUBLISHING

COPYRIGHT © 2025.

ALL RIGHTS RESERVED.

CONTENTS

WHATS INSIDE

1. HISTORY : PAGE 4
2. RULES : PAGE 9
3. WHAT IT TAKES : PAGE 13
4. KIT : PAGE 23
5. STADIUMS : PAGE 26
6. CLUBS : PAGE 42
7. PLAYERS : PAGE 52
8. RIVALRIES : PAGE 57
9. COMPETITIONS : PAGE 65
10. GAMES : PAGE 79
11. RECORDS : PAGE 86
12. QUIZ PAGE 91

INTRO

WELCOME TO SOCCER HISTORY

Soccer isn't just a game—it's a global obsession, a sport filled with incredible history, legendary players, and unbelievable moments. From the biggest stadiums to the craziest matches, from record-breaking goals to fierce rivalries, this book is packed with everything a young soccer fan needs to know!

Inside, you'll explore how soccer began, discover the rules of the game, and learn what it takes to become a star. You'll dive into tactics and formations, visit the world's most famous stadiums, and meet the greatest clubs and players in history. Plus, we've included mind-blowing fun facts, weird records, and a quiz to test your soccer knowledge!

So lace up your cleats, step onto the pitch and get ready for an exciting journey through the world's favorite sport. Whether you dream of scoring the winning goal or just love watching the game, this book is made for you. Let's kick off!

HISTORY

HISTORY AND ORIGINS OF THE BEAUTIFUL GAME

THAT'S HISTORY!

ANCIENT TIMES

THE ORIGINS OF THE GAME

- CONSIDERED ONE OF THE EARLIEST FORMS OF SOCCER
- PLAYERS KICKED A LEATHER BALL THROUGH A SMALL GOAL.
- IT STARTED AROUND 2,000 YEARS AGO IN CHINA DURING THE HAN DYNASTY.
- "CUJU" LITERALLY MEANS "KICK THE BALL."

- THIS ROMAN BALL GAME INVOLVED TWO TEAMS TRYING TO KEEP THE BALL ON THEIR SIDE OF THE FIELD.
- PLAYERS COULD BOTH CARRY AND KICK THE BALL, AND IT COULD GET QUITE ROUGH!

- DURING THE MIDDLE AGES, VILLAGES HELD HUGE FOOTBALL MATCHES WHERE LARGE GROUPS OF PEOPLE WOULD TRY TO MOVE THE BALL—BY KICKING OR CARRYING IT—ACROSS TOWN.
- RULES VARIED FROM PLACE TO PLACE, AND GAMES COULD BE CHAOTIC, WITH ENTIRE COMMUNITIES JOINING IN.

CHANGING TIMES

THE BIRTH OF MODERN SOCCER (1800S)

DIFFERENT SCHOOL RULES

By the 1800s in England, schools and clubs had different ways of playing.

Some allowed players to use their hands, which led to what we now call rugby.

Others preferred strictly kicking the ball—this would become modern soccer.

THE 1863 MEETING

Representatives from several English schools and clubs gathered in London to create a standard set of rules.

This is when the Football Association (**THE FA**) was formed.

They decided hands would not be allowed (except by the goalkeeper), and tackling below the knees was not allowed.

These rules were written down for the first time.

MODERN TIMES

MODERN ERA INNOVATIONS

VAR (2010)
VAR HELPS REFEREES REVIEW BIG DECISIONS LIKE GOALS, PENALTIES, AND RED CARDS USING VIDEO REPLAYS. IF NEEDED, THE REFEREE CAN CHECK A SCREEN ON THE FIELD TO MAKE THE RIGHT CALL.

GOAL-LINE TECHNOLOGY (2012)
BEFORE THIS, REFEREES HAD TO GUESS IF A BALL CROSSED THE GOAL LINE. NOW, CAMERAS AND SENSORS INSTANTLY DETECT GOALS AND SEND A SIGNAL TO THE REFEREE'S WATCH, MAKING SURE EVERY GOAL COUNTS!

SEMI-AUTOMATED OFFSIDE (2022)
TO SPEED UP OFFSIDE DECISIONS, FIFA INTRODUCED A SYSTEM USING AI AND LIMB-TRACKING SENSORS. IT DETECTS OFFSIDES REDUCING MISTAKES AND DELAYS.

SMART MATCH BALLS (2023)
THESE HIGH-TECH BALLS HAVE TINY SENSORS INSIDE THAT TRACK EVERY TOUCH IN REAL-TIME. THEY HELP REFEREES MAKE MORE ACCURATE OFFSIDE AND HANDBALL DECISIONS DURING A GAME.

DID YOU KNOW THE FA CUP WENT MISSING AND WAS FOUND BY A DOG?
*MORE ON THAT LATER

8

RULES

TODAYS RULES

THE LAWS OF THE GAME

9

BASICS

SOME BASIC RULES OF THE GAME

- Two teams of 11 players (including a goalkeeper).

- The goal is to score by kicking the ball into the opponent's net.

- Matches last 90 minutes (two 45-minute halves + extra time if needed).

- The ball must completely cross the goal line to count as a goal.

- The game continues unless the referee stops play for fouls, offsides, or out-of-bounds.

- No handball (except for goalkeepers in their own penalty area).

- No tripping, pushing, or dangerous play—these result in free kicks or penalties.

- A yellow card is a warning; a red card means ejection from the game.

- Most competitions allow 3-5 substitutions per team.

- If a game ends in a tie during knockout rounds, it may go to extra time (30 minutes) or a penalty shootout.

RULES

IMPORTANT EARLY RULE CHANGES

- **Offside Rule (1863):** Early offside rules said that any attacking player ahead of the ball could not receive a pass. This rule has changed multiple times to make the game more exciting.

- **Introduction of Referees (1870s-1880s):** At first, teams tried to settle disagreements on their own. As the game became more popular, official referees were brought in to enforce the rules.

- **Goal Nets (1891):** Before nets, it was sometimes hard to tell if the ball actually went into the goal. Adding nets made it easier for referees to see when a goal was scored.

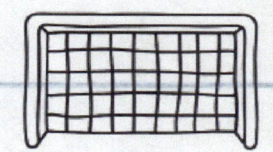

- **Penalty Kick (1891):** If a defender broke the rules close to their own goal, the other team got a "free shot" at the goal from a set distance. This was introduced to discourage foul play near the goal.

RULES

20TH CENTURY CHANGES

- **Red and Yellow Cards (1970):** The idea of showing cards to players who misbehave came about during the 1970 FIFA World Cup. A yellow card is a warning, and a red card means you're sent out of the game.

- **Substitutions:** Over time, the number of players who could be swapped in and out of a match changed. In the early years, no substitutions were allowed at all. Today, leagues typically allow three to five substitutions, depending on competition rules.

- **Offside Tweaks:** The offside rule was changed many times to ensure attacking play stayed exciting. Today, you are offside if you are nearer to the opponent's goal line than both the ball and the second-last defender (usually the last defender is the goalkeeper).

WHAT IT TAKES

TACTICS AND PLAYER ATTRIBUTES NEEDED TO BE A STAR

TACTICS

Soccer isn't just about scoring goals—it's a game of strategy, skill, and smart decision-making!

Teams use tactics to attack, defend, and control the match, with formations shaping how they play.
But no matter the game plan, the best players stand out with talent, intelligence, and determination.

A great player doesn't just follow tactics—they make them work with skill, effort, and a winning mindset!

"TO BE A TOP PLAYER, YOU HAVE TO COMBINE PHYSICAL POWER, TECHNICAL ABILITY, AND MENTAL STRENGTH. YOU MUST TRAIN HARD, STAY FOCUSED, AND ALWAYS BELIEVE IN YOURSELF."

— ZINEDINE ZIDANE

SOCCER BRAIN

LEARN ABOUT THE TOP MENTAL ATTRIBUTES NEEDED AT THE TOP LEVEL.

ANTICIPATION
Guessing what will happen next and acting first.

BRAVERY
Taking risks and never backing down—no matter the challenge.

COMPOSURE
Staying calm under pressure, making smart decisions, and not panicking

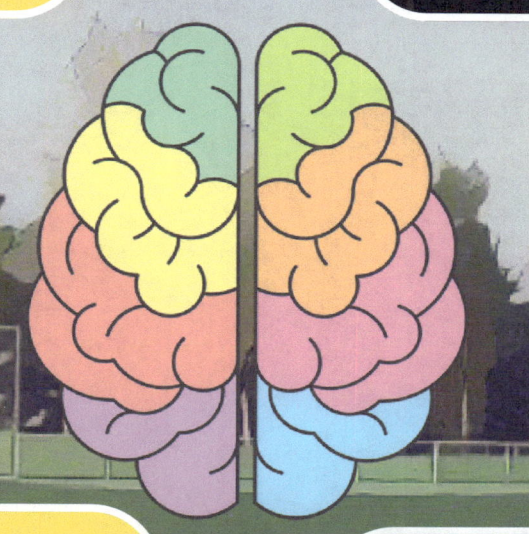

FLAIR
Playing with skill, creativity and style—using tricks and smart moves to beat opponents!

OFF THE BALL
Moving into space, making smart runs, and staying ready to help your team—even without the ball

CONCENTRATION
Staying focused, alert, and ready for every pass, tackle, and goal-scoring chance!

VISION
Seeing the game before it happens—spotting passes, creating chances, and making smart plays

DETERMINATION
Never giving up—fighting for every ball, chasing every chance, and pushing through challenges!.

SOCCER BODY

LEARN ABOUT THE TOP PHYSICAL ATTRIBUTES NEEDED AT THE TOP LEVEL.

STAMINA
KEEPING YOUR ENERGY HIGH, RUNNING STRONG, AND STAYING SHARP FOR THE WHOLE GAME!

STRENGTH
USING POWER TO HOLD OFF OPPONENTS, WIN TACKLES, AND STAY STRONG ON THE BALL!

PACE
SPEED TO SPRINT PAST DEFENDERS, CHASE THE BALL, AND BREAK AWAY ON THE ATTACK!

AGILITY
QUICK TURNS, SHARP MOVES, AND FAST REACTIONS TO DODGE DEFENDERS AND STAY IN CONTROL!

BALANCE
STAYING STEADY ON YOUR FEET, CONTROLLING THE BALL, AND STAYING STRONG AGAINST CHALLENGES!

ACCELERATION
EXPLODING INTO SPEED QUICKLY TO BEAT DEFENDERS AND REACH THE BALL FIRST!

NATURAL FITNESS
THE ABILITY TO STAY STRONG, RECOVER QUICKLY, AND KEEP GOING GAME AFTER GAME!

JUMPING REACH
LEAPING HIGH TO WIN HEADERS, DEFEND CROSSES, AND SCORE GOALS IN THE AIR!

SOCCER TECHNICALS

LEARN ABOUT THE TOP TECHNICAL ATTRIBUTES NEEDED AT THE TOP LEVEL.

CROSSING
SENDING THE BALL INTO THE BOX TO SET UP TEAMMATES FOR A GOAL!

PASSING
SENDING THE BALL ACCURATELY TO TEAMMATES TO KEEP POSSESSION AND CREATE CHANCES!

TACKLING
WINNING THE BALL BACK WITH STRONG, CLEAN CHALLENGES TO STOP OPPONENTS!

DRIBBLING
MOVING PAST DEFENDERS WITH SKILL, CONTROL, AND QUICK FOOTWORK!

FIRST TOUCH
CONTROLLING THE BALL SMOOTHLY TO KEEP POSSESSION AND MAKE YOUR NEXT MOVE!

FINISHING
STRIKING THE BALL WITH ACCURACY AND POWER TO SCORE GOALS!

HEADING
USING YOUR HEAD TO PASS, CLEAR, OR SCORE GOALS WITH POWER AND CONTROL!

MARKING
STAYING CLOSE TO YOUR OPPONENT TO BLOCK PASSES, STOP RUNS, AND WIN THE BALL!

FORMATIONS

MOST USED FORMATIONS

442

BALANCED

ADVANTAGES	DISADVANTAGES
 EASY TO UNDERSTAND TWO STRIKERS CREATE MULTIPLE SCORING OPTIONS. BALANCED FOCUS ON BOTH ATTACK AND DEFENSE.	PREDICTABLE SHAPE—OPPONENTS KNOW WHAT TO EXPECT. RELIES HEAVILY ON STRONG WINGERS FOR WIDTH. LESS FLEXIBILITY FOR TACTICAL CHANGES DURING A MATCH.

433

ATTACKING

ADVANTAGES	DISADVANTAGES
 STRONG ATTACKING FORCE. WINGERS STRETCH THE FIELD, CREATING SPACE FOR TEAMMATES. EFFECTIVE HIGH-PRESSING STRATEGY	REQUIRES HIGH FITNESS LEVELS. GAPS CAN APPEAR IF PRESSING IS NOT WELL-ORGANIZED. THE LONE CENTRAL STRIKER CAN BECOME ISOLATED IF WINGERS DON'T SUPPORT.

FORMATIONS

MOST USED FORMATIONS

DEFENSIVE

532

ADVANTAGES	DISADVANTAGES
FIVE DEFENDERS MAKE IT TOUGH TO BREAK THROUGH. WINGBACKS PROVIDE WIDTH AND SUPPORT IN ATTACK. BALANCED THREE MIDFIELDERS HELP CONTROL POSSESSION AND BREAK UP PLAY	NO WINGERS MAKE WIDE ATTACKS HARDER. WINGBACKS MUST CONSTANTLY RUN BACK AND FORTH. (HIGH FITNESS DEMAND) FEWER ATTACKERS ONLY TWO STRIKERS CAN LIMIT GOAL-SCORING CHANCES.

CONTROL

352

ADVANTAGES	DISADVANTAGES
CONTROL POSSESSION AND DOMINATE THE CENTER. WING-BACKS CAN BOTH DEFEND AND ATTACK, ADDING SURPRISE TACTICS. FLEXIBLE SHAPE.	REQUIRES EXCELLENT COMMUNICATION AMONG THE THREE CENTRAL DEFENDERS. DEMANDS HIGH STAMINA FROM WING-BACKS. CAN BE COMPLICATED FOR LESS EXPERIENCED TEAMS TO EXECUTE WELL.

SET PIECES

SOCCER PLAYS TAKEN AFTER A STOPPAGE TO CREATE SCORING CHANCES!

Throw-in
When the ball goes out on the sideline, the other team throws it back in.

Corner kick
If the defending team last touches the ball before it crosses their own goal line, the other team gets a kick from the corner.

Goal kick
If the attacking team last touches it before going over the goal line, the defending team kicks it back into play.

Penalty kick:
Awarded if a foul occurs inside the penalty area.

Drop Ball:
Restarts play after an unintended stoppage. The referee drops the ball to the last team that touched it, with opponents 4 meters away.

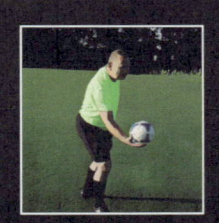

POSITIONS

WHERE TO PLAY

ST — FORWARD/STRIKER = MAIN GOAL SCORER

CM — CENTRAL MIDFIELDER = LINKS DEFENSE AND ATTACK; CONTROLS THE FLOW OF THE GAME

CB — CENTRAL DEFENDER = PROTECTS THE GOAL BY STOPPING OPPOSING ATTACKERS

GK — GOALKEEPER = THE ONLY PLAYER ALLOWED TO USE HANDS (INSIDE THE PENALTY BOX)

FB — FULL BACK = DEFENDER THAT PATROLS THE SIDELINES, OFTEN SUPPORTS IN ATTACK

W — WINGER = STAYS WIDE TO STRETCH THE FIELD

POSITIONS

FAMOUS CURRENT AND LEGENDARY PLAYERS IN EACH POSITION

FORWARDS : MESSI  · RONALDO  · HAALAND  · MBAPPE

MIDFIELDERS : RONALDINHO  · BELLINGHAM  · ZIDANE  · DE BRUYNE

DEFENDERS : VAN DIJK  · PUYOL  · RAMOS  · CANNAVARO

GOALKEEPERS : BUFFON  · NEUER  · CECH  · CASILLAS

22

KIT

THE HISTORY WHAT YOU NEED TO WEAR TO PLAY

Imagine playing soccer in a wool sweater, long trousers, and heavy boots—sounds impossible, right? But that's how players dressed over 100 years ago!

Back then, there were no flashy jerseys or lightweight cleats. Teams wore whatever they had, sometimes even school uniforms! But as soccer grew, so did the need for better, faster, and more comfortable gear.

From baggy cotton shirts to high-tech jerseys, and from heavy boots to speed-boosting cleats, soccer kits have come a long way. So, how did we go from old-school wool to today's sleek designs? Let's find out!

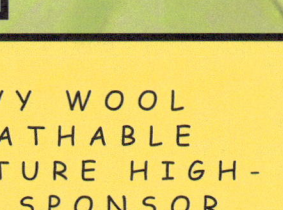

Soccer jerseys evolved from heavy wool shirts in the 1800s to light, breathable fabrics by the 1970s, and today feature high-tech materials, bold designs, and sponsor logos, blending performance with style.

23

KIT

THE HISTORY OF WHAT YOU NEED TO WEAR TO PLAY

SHIN PADS WERE FIRST USED IN THE 1800S, INSPIRED BY CRICKET LEG GUARDS, AND WERE MADE OF HEAVY LEATHER. BY THE 20TH CENTURY, THEY BECAME LIGHTER AND MORE FLEXIBLE, AND TODAY'S VERSIONS USE HIGH-TECH MATERIALS LIKE CARBON FIBER FOR MAXIMUM PROTECTION AND COMFORT.

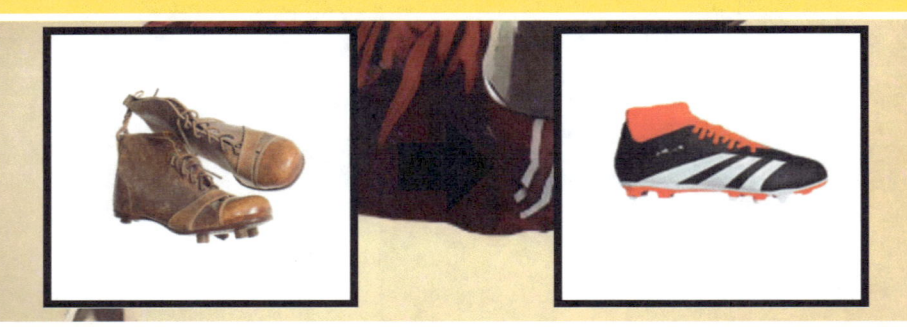

SOCCER BOOTS BEGAN AS HEAVY LEATHER WORK BOOTS IN THE 1800S, EVOLVED INTO LIGHTER DESIGNS WITH REPLACEABLE STUDS IN THE 1950S, AND BY THE 1990S, BECAME SLEEK, COLORFUL, AND BUILT FOR SPEED. TODAY'S CLEATS USE HIGH-TECH MATERIALS FOR BETTER CONTROL, TRACTION, AND COMFORT.

KIT

THE HISTORY WHAT YOU NEED TO WEAR TO PLAY

GOALKEEPER GLOVES WERE RARELY USED BEFORE THE 1960S, WITH KEEPERS RELYING ON BARE HANDS. IN THE 1970S, GLOVES WITH BASIC PADDING APPEARED, AND BY THE 1990S, THEY FEATURED GRIPPY LATEX PALMS AND FINGER PROTECTION. TODAY'S GLOVES USE HIGH-TECH MATERIALS FOR MAXIMUM GRIP, SHOCK ABSORPTION, AND FLEXIBILITY.

SOCCER BALLS STARTED AS PIG BLADDERS WRAPPED IN LEATHER, BECAME STITCHED LEATHER BALLS IN THE EARLY 1900S, AND EVOLVED INTO WATERPROOF, SYNTHETIC DESIGNS BY THE 1970S, LEADING TO TODAY'S HIGH-TECH, AERODYNAMIC MATCH BALLS.

25

STADIUMS

LEARN ABOUT FAMOUS SOCCER STADIUMS FROM AROUND THE WORLD

IT'S OUR HOME!

A STADIUM AS MORE THAN JUST A PLACE—IT'S A FORTRESS AND A HOME FOR THE CLUB AND ITS FANS.

STADIUMS

THE MOST EXPENSIVE STADIUMS IN THE WORLD

ALLIANZ ARENA (75,000) MUNICH, GERMANY BAYERN MUNICH	$380M
STAMFORD BRIDGE (40,173) LONDON, ENGLAND. CHELSEA F.C.	$400M
ETIHAD STADIUM (53,400) MANCHESTER, ENGLAND MANCHESTER CITY	$600M
CAPE TOWN STADIUM (55,000) CAPE TOWN, SOUTH AFRICA WORLD CUP GAMES	$600M
PUSKÁS ARÉNA (67,215) BUDAPEST, HUNGARY HUNGARY NATIONAL FOOTBALL TEAM	$610M

STADIUMS

THE MOST EXPENSIVE STADIUMS IN THE WORLD

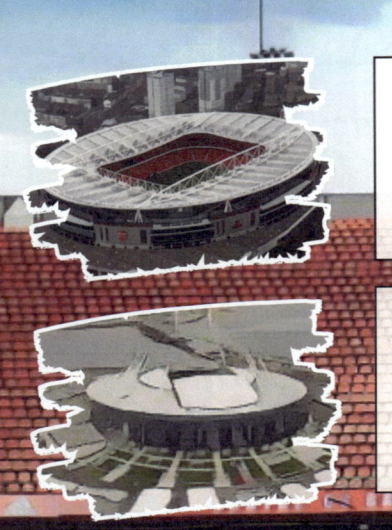

EMIRATES STADIUM (60,704) LONDON, ENGLAND ARSENAL — **$750M**

KRESTOVSKY STADIUM (68,000) SAINT PETERSBURG, RUSSIA FC ZENIT SAINT PETERSBURG — **$1.1B**

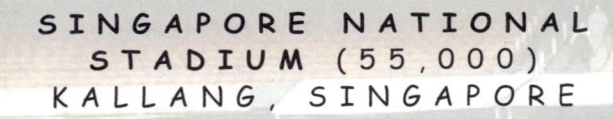

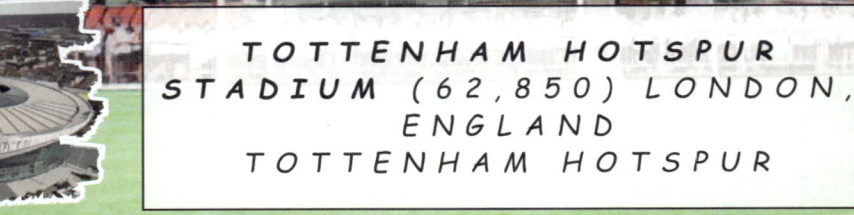

SINGAPORE NATIONAL STADIUM (55,000) KALLANG, SINGAPORE — **$1.31B**

TOTTENHAM HOTSPUR STADIUM (62,850) LONDON, ENGLAND TOTTENHAM HOTSPUR — **$1.33B**

WEMBLEY STADIUM (90,000) LONDON, ENGLAND ENGLAND NATION TEAM — **$1.5B**

STADIUMS

LEGENDARY STADIUMS ACROSS THE WORLD

LEGENDARY

📍 OLD TRAFFORD , ENGLAND

OLD TRAFFORD, OFTEN CALLED "THE THEATRE OF DREAMS," IS THE ICONIC HOME OF MANCHESTER UNITED FOOTBALL CLUB.

OPENED: FEBRUARY 19, 1910

HOME TO: MANCHESTER UNITED F.C.

CAPACITY: APPROXIMATELY 74,310 SEATS

KNOWN FOR: ITS RICH HISTORY, HOSTING NUMEROUS MEMORABLE MATCHES, AND BEING ONE OF THE MOST RENOWNED FOOTBALL STADIUMS GLOBALLY.

STADIUMS

LEGENDARY STADIUMS ACROSS THE WORLD

LEGENDARY

📍 ANFIELD, ENGLAND

ANFIELD IS THE HISTORIC HOME OF LIVERPOOL FOOTBALL CLUB, RENOWNED FOR ITS PASSIONATE ATMOSPHERE AND RICH HERITAGE.

OPENED: 1884

HOME TO: LIVERPOOL F.C. SINCE 1892

CAPACITY: 61,276 SEATS

KNOWN FOR: THE ICONIC SPION KOP STAND, FAMOUS FOR ITS VIBRANT SUPPORTERS AND THE STIRRING ANTHEM "YOU'LL NEVER WALK ALONE."

STADIUMS

LEGENDARY STADIUMS ACROSS THE WORLD

LEGENDARY

CELTIC PARK, SCOTLAND

With its electric atmosphere and passionate supporters, it's one of the most intimidating stadiums in Europe, especially on famous European nights!

OPENED: 1892

HOME TO: CELTIC F.C.

CAPACITY: 60,411 SEATS

KNOWN FOR: Its unmatched atmosphere, legendary European nights, and the deafening roar of the Celtic faithful, making it one of the most intimidating stadiums in Europe.

STADIUMS

LEGENDARY STADIUMS ACROSS THE WORLD

LEGENDARY

SAN SIRO, ITALY

Home to both AC Milan and Inter Milan, this legendary venue has seen countless epic matches, roaring fans, and unforgettable moments in Serie A and the Champions League!

Opened: 1926

Home to: AC Milan & Inter Milan

Capacity: 75,817 seats

Known for: Its towering stands, fierce Milan derby battles, and legendary European nights, making it one of the most iconic stadiums in world football.

STADIUMS

LEGENDARY STADIUMS ACROSS THE WORLD

LEGENDARY

CAMP NOU, SPAIN

CAMP NOU IS THE ULTIMATE STAGE FOR FOOTBALLING GREATNESS. WITH ITS ROARING CROWDS AND RICH HISTORY, THIS ICONIC STADIUM HAS BEEN THE HOME OF BARCELONA'S GOLDEN ERAS,

OPENED: 1957

HOME TO: FC BARCELONA

LOCATION: BARCELONA, SPAIN

CAPACITY: 99,354 SEATS

KNOWN FOR: BEING EUROPE'S LARGEST STADIUM, HOSTING MAGICAL NIGHTS OF TIKI-TAKA FOOTBALL, AND WITNESSING THE BRILLIANCE OF LEGENDS LIKE MESSI, CRUYFF, AND RONALDINHO.

DID YOU KNOW?

DID YOU KNOW ?
YOU CAN FIT 238 BUSES INSIDE A STANDARD SOCCER FIELD

STADIUMS

LEGENDARY STADIUMS ACROSS THE WORLD

LEGENDARY

SANTIAGO BERNABÉU, SPAIN

THE SANTIAGO BERNABÉU IS A CATHEDRAL OF FOOTBALL, WHERE REAL MADRID'S TRIUMPHS, EPIC COMEBACKS, AND LEGENDARY MOMENTS HAVE MADE IT ONE OF THE GREATEST STADIUMS IN THE WORLD!

OPENED: 1947

HOME TO: REAL MADRID C.F.

CAPACITY: 81,044 SEATS

KNOWN FOR: HOSTING COUNTLESS CHAMPIONS LEAGUE NIGHTS, BEING THE STAGE FOR SOME OF THE GREATEST PLAYERS IN HISTORY, AND UNDERGOING A MASSIVE MODERN TRANSFORMATION TO BECOME ONE OF THE MOST ADVANCED STADIUMS IN THE WORLD

STADIUMS

THE MOST REMOTE STADIUM IN THE WORLD

COOLEST

📍 HENNINGSVAER STADION, LOFOTEN, NORWAY

FORGET GIANT STADIUMS—HENNINGSVÆR STADION IS PURE MAGIC. NESTLED ON A REMOTE ISLAND IN NORWAY,

HOME TO: HENNINGSVÆR IL (AMATEUR AND LOCAL TEAMS)

CAPACITY: NO OFFICIAL STANDS, BUT SURROUNDED BY BREATHTAKING SCENERY

KNOWN FOR: ITS UNREAL LOCATION ON A TINY ROCKY ISLAND, SURROUNDED BY THE NORWEGIAN SEA AND TOWERING MOUNTAINS, MAKING IT ONE OF THE MOST PICTURESQUE SOCCER FIELDS ON EARTH.

STADIUMS

THE HIGHEST SOCCER STADIUM IN THE WORLD

COOLEST

OTTMAR HITZFELD STADIUM, SWITZERLAND

Perched high in the Swiss Alps, Ottmar Hitzfeld Stadium is a one-of-a-kind football pitch. With no roads leading to it, players and fans must hike or take a cable car just to reach the game—talk about home-field advantage!

OPENED: N/A (Used for local matches and training)

HOME TO: FC Gspon (Amateur team)

CAPACITY: 200 seats

KNOWN FOR: Being the highest soccer stadium in Europe, sitting at an incredible 2,000 meters (6,561 feet) above sea level, surrounded by breathtaking Swiss Alps.

STADIUMS

A FLOATING STADIUM!

COOLEST

🚩 **THE FLOAT. MARINA BAY (SINGAPORE)**

SITTING RIGHT ON THE WATER, THE FLOAT @ MARINA BAY IS A ONE-OF-A-KIND STADIUM, WHERE PLAYERS COMPETE ON A FLOATING PITCH WITH THE SINGAPORE SKYLINE GLITTERING IN THE BACKGROUND.

OPENED: 2007

HOME TO: USED FOR VARIOUS EVENTS, INCLUDING SOCCER MATCHES

CAPACITY: 27,000 SEATS

KNOWN FOR: BEING THE WORLD'S LARGEST FLOATING STADIUM, WITH A 100% STEEL PITCH BUILT OVER WATER, CREATING A BREATHTAKING BACKDROP OF SINGAPORE'S SKYLINE.

STADIUMS

A STADIUM ON TOP OF A SKY SCRAPER!

COOLEST

📍 THE ADIDAS FUTSAL PARK, TOYKO, JAPAN

IMAGINE PLAYING SOCCER ABOVE THE CITY, SURROUNDED BY THE BRIGHT LIGHTS OF TOKYO! ADIDAS FUTSAL PARK IS A ONE-OF-A-KIND ROOFTOP PITCH, PROVING THAT YOU DON'T NEED A HUGE STADIUM TO EXPERIENCE THE MAGIC OF THE GAME!

OPENED: 2001

HOME TO: AMATEUR FUTSAL PLAYERS AND LOCAL LEAGUES

CAPACITY: SMALL, RECREATIONAL USE ONLY

KNOWN FOR: BEING A FUTSAL PITCH BUILT ON TOP OF A SKYSCRAPER, OFFERING A BREATHTAKING VIEW OF TOKYO, AND ONCE SITTING ABOVE THE SHIBUYA TRAIN STATION, ONE OF THE BUSIEST PLACES IN THE WORLD.

STADIUMS

A STADIUM BY THE SEA!

COOLEST

EIDI STADIUM, FAROE ISLANDS

NESTLED ON THE RUGGED COASTLINE OF THE FAROE ISLANDS, EIDI STADIUM OFFERS A STUNNING, YET DANGEROUS SETTING FOR SOCCER. WITH THE OCEAN JUST METERS AWAY, ANY MISPLACED SHOT COULD SEND THE BALL STRAIGHT INTO THE SEA—SO AIM CAREFULLY!

OPENED: N/A (USED FOR LOCAL MATCHES)

HOME TO: LOCAL TEAMS IN THE FAROE ISLANDS

CAPACITY: SMALL, WITH NO OFFICIAL STANDS

KNOWN FOR: ITS BREATHTAKING LOCATION ON A CLIFFSIDE, SURROUNDED BY THE NORTH ATLANTIC OCEAN, MAKING IT ONE OF THE MOST SCENIC AND REMOTE SOCCER FIELDS IN THE WORLD.

STADIUMS

THE OLDEST STADIUM IN THE WORLD

OLDEST

📍 SHEFFIELD, ENGLAND

Sandygate Road isn't just a soccer field—it's where the sport's journey started! As the oldest football ground in the world, it has stood for over 200 years, reminding us of where the beautiful game all began!

OPENED: 1804

HOME TO: HALLAM F.C. (SINCE 1860)

CAPACITY: 700 SEATS

KNOWN FOR: BEING OFFICIALLY RECOGNIZED AS THE WORLD'S OLDEST FOOTBALL GROUND, HOSTING THE FIRST-EVER INTER-CLUB SOCCER MATCH IN 1860 BETWEEN HALLAM F.C. AND SHEFFIELD F.C.

STADIUMS

THE MOST FAMOUS SOCCER CLUBS WORLDWIDE

Some soccer clubs aren't just teams—they're global icons! With millions of fans, historic victories, and legendary players, these clubs have dominated the sport for decades.

Whether it's Real Madrid's trophies, Barcelona's tiki-taka, or Manchester United's legendary history, these teams are known everywhere. Let's dive into the biggest and most famous clubs on the planet!

CLUBS

BEST CLUBS WORLDWIDE

NAME = PSG

COUNTRY = FRANCE

FOUNDED = 1970

STADIUM = PARC DES PRINCES

DOMESTIC CUPS = 14

EUROPEAN CUPS = 0

BEST RECORD = CHAMPIONS LEAGUE FINALISTS 2020

PSG is the newest powerhouse on this list, but they've quickly become one of the biggest clubs in the world! Founded in 1970, PSG has dominated French soccer, winning multiple league titles while bringing in some of the biggest superstars.

With Kylian Mbappé, Neymar, and Messi playing for them, PSG has taken over the Parc des Princes stadium with their exciting, attacking football. They are still chasing their first Champions League title, but with their superstar lineup, it's only a matter of time before they reach the top!

CLUBS

FIRST CLUB TO WIN ALL THREE MAJOR EUROPEAN COMPETITIONS—THE CHAMPIONS LEAGUE, EUROPA LEAGUE, AND CUP WINNERS' CUP!

NAME = JUVENTUS

COUNTRY = ITALY

FOUNDED = 1897

STADIUM = ALLIANZ STADIUM

DOMESTIC CUPS = 15

EUROPEAN CUPS = 2

BEST RECORD = NINE CONSECUTIVE SERIE A TITLES

Founded in 1897, Juventus is the most successful club in Italian soccer history. Nicknamed "The Old Lady", they have dominated Serie A, winning more league titles than any other team. Their famous black and white striped jerseys have been worn by legends like Alessandro Del Piero, Gianluigi Buffon, and Cristiano Ronaldo.

Juventus is known for their strong defense, tactical brilliance, and never-give-up attitude. They have a rich history in European football, winning two Champions League titles, and their home stadium, Allianz Stadium, is a fortress for their passionate fans.

The club has achieved incredible success, including an unmatched nine straight Serie A titles from 2011 to 2020.

CLUBS

Liverpool has won more Champions League titles (6) than any other English club!

Name = Liverpool

Country = England

Founded = 1892

Stadium = Anfield

Domestic Cups = 8

European Cups = 6

Best Record = Treble in 2020, winning the Premier League, UEFA Champions League, and FIFA Club World Cup.

Nicknamed "The Reds", they are famous for their attacking football, legendary comebacks, and passionate fans who fill Anfield with their iconic anthem, "You'll Never Walk Alone."

Liverpool has dominated both English and European soccer, winning multiple league titles and six Champions League trophies. Legends like Steven Gerrard, Kenny Dalglish, and Mohamed Salah have all worn the famous red jersey, leading Liverpool to unforgettable moments.

After decades of waiting, Liverpool finally won the Premier League in 2020, completing a historic treble with the Champions League and FIFA Club World Cup. With their rich history and never-give-up attitude, Liverpool continues to be one of the most feared teams in the world!

DID YOU KNOW?

AT THE ST PAULI STADIUM IN GERMANY. BRATWURSTS(SAUSAGES) ARE DELIVERED TO SEATS BY TRAIN!

CLUBS

Barcelona's motto is "Més que un club", which means "More than a club" in Catalan!

Name = Barcelona

Country = Spain

Founded = 1899

Stadium = Camp Nou

Domestic Cups = 31

European Cups = 5

Best Record = Treble in 2009 winning La Liga, Copa del Rey, and the UEFA Champions League.

Founded in 1899, Barcelona is one of the most exciting teams in soccer history, famous for their tiki-taka passing style. They believe in playing beautiful, attacking soccer, and their fans expect nothing less!

Some of the greatest players ever have worn the famous blue and red jersey, including Lionel Messi, Ronaldinho, and Johan Cruyff. Their home, the Camp Nou, is one of the biggest stadiums in the world, where over 90,000 fans chant and cheer their team to victory!

Barcelona also takes pride in developing young stars through La Masia, their world-famous academy that produced legends like Messi, Xavi, and Iniesta.

CLUBS

Bayern Munich achieved an unprecedented 11 consecutive Bundesliga titles from the 2012-13 to the 2022-23 seasons.

Name = Bayern Munich

Country = Germany

Founded = 1900

Stadium = Allianz Arena

Domestic Cups = 20

European Cups = 6

Best Record = Secured a sextuple in 2020, winning the Bundesliga, DFB-Pokal, UEFA Champions League, DFL-Supercup, UEFA Super Cup, and FIFA Club World Cup.

No team dominates German soccer like Bayern Munich! Founded in 1900, Bayern has won more Bundesliga titles than any other team, making them the undisputed kings of German football."

Bayern is known for its powerful attacking play, solid defense, and never-satisfied hunger for trophies. Legends like Franz Beckenbauer, Gerd Müller, and Robert Lewandowski have worn the famous red jersey, helping Bayern win multiple Champions League titles.

Their home, the Allianz Arena, is famous for its glowing red lights at night, making it one of the coolest stadiums in the world. Whether in Germany or in Europe, when Bayern Munich plays, they play to win it all!

CLUBS

ONLY ENGLISH CLUB TO HAVE WON THE PREMIER LEAGUE TITLE THREE CONSECUTIVE TIMES ON TWO SEPARATE OCCASIONS.

NAME = MANCHESTER UTD

COUNTRY = ENGLAND

FOUNDED = 1900

STADIUM = OLD TRAFFORD

DOMESTIC CUPS = 12

EUROPEAN CUPS = 3

BEST RECORD = THE TREBLE IN THE 1998-1999 SEASON, WINNING THE PREMIER LEAGUE, FA CUP, AND UEFA CHAMPIONS LEAGUE.

FOUNDED IN 1878, MANCHESTER UNITED IS ONE OF THE BIGGEST CLUBS IN ENGLAND AND THE WORLD! THEIR FAMOUS OLD TRAFFORD STADIUM, NICKNAMED THE "THEATRE OF DREAMS", HAS SEEN SOME OF THE GREATEST MOMENTS IN SOCCER HISTORY.

UNITED IS KNOWN FOR THEIR ATTACKING FOOTBALL, NEVER-SAY-DIE ATTITUDE, AND INCREDIBLE COMEBACKS. LEGENDARY MANAGER SIR ALEX FERGUSON LED THEM TO 13 PREMIER LEAGUE TITLES, WHILE STARS LIKE DAVID BECKHAM, CRISTIANO RONALDO, AND ERIC CANTONA BECAME LEGENDS WEARING THE FAMOUS RED JERSEY.

ONE OF THEIR MOST UNFORGETTABLE MOMENTS CAME IN 1999, WHEN UNITED SCORED TWO GOALS IN STOPPAGE TIME TO WIN THE CHAMPIONS LEAGUE FINAL, COMPLETING AN INCREDIBLE TREBLE (THREE MAJOR TROPHIES IN ONE SEASON)!

CLUBS

THE ONLY CLUB TO WIN THE UEFA CHAMPIONS LEAGUE THREE TIMES IN A ROW ON TWO SEPARATE OCCASIONS

NAME = REAL MADRID

COUNTRY = SPAIN

FOUNDED = 1902

STADIUM = SANTIAGO BERNABÉU

DOMESTIC CUPS = 19

EUROPEAN CUPS = 15

BEST RECORD = ACHIEVED A RECORD FIVE CONSECUTIVE EUROPEAN CUP (NOW CHAMPIONS LEAGUE) TITLES FROM 1956 TO 1960.

When it comes to winning trophies, no club does it better than Real Madrid! Founded in 1902, this Spanish giant has dominated soccer for over a century, collecting more Champions League titles than any other team.

Their famous all-white uniforms have been worn by some of the greatest players in history, including Cristiano Ronaldo, Zinedine Zidane, and Alfredo Di Stéfano.

With their famous Santiago Bernabéu stadium packed with roaring fans, Real Madrid is known for huge comebacks, last-minute goals, and magical moments. If there's one thing you should know about Madrid, it's this—they never give up!

LONGEST UNBEATEN RUN!

AC MILAN WENT 58 GAMES WITHOUT LOSING (1991-1993).

THAT'S ALMOST TWO WHOLE SEASONS!

LEGENDARY PLAYERS

BEST PLAYERS OF ALL TIME

SOME PLAYERS DON'T JUST PLAY SOCCER—THEY CHANGE THE GAME FOREVER. WITH UNBELIEVABLE SKILL, RECORD-BREAKING ACHIEVEMENTS, AND MOMENTS OF PURE MAGIC,

THESE LEGENDS HAVE LEFT THEIR MARK ON HISTORY. WHETHER THROUGH JAW-DROPPING GOALS, INCREDIBLE LEADERSHIP, OR UNFORGETTABLE PERFORMANCES ON THE BIGGEST STAGE,

THESE PLAYERS HAVE INSPIRED GENERATIONS. THEIR NAMES ARE REMEMBERED NOT JUST FOR WHAT THEY WON, BUT FOR HOW THEY MADE THE WORLD FALL IN LOVE WITH SOCCER!

PLAYERS

BEST PLAYERS OF ALL TIME

PELE

THE KING OF SOCCER

THE KING OF SOCCER, WON **3** WORLD CUPS, **6** BRAZILIAN LEAGUE TITLES WITH SANTOS, AND SCORED OVER **1,000** GOALS.

THE MAGICIAN

MARADONA

A MAGICIAN WITH THE BALL, LED ARGENTINA TO WORLD CUP GLORY IN 1986, WON **2** SERIE A TITLES WITH NAPOLI, SCORED THE "GOAL OF THE CENTURY", AND NETTED 345 CAREER GOALS (INCLUDING 34 FOR ARGENTINA).

PLAYERS

BEST PLAYERS OF ALL TIME

RONALDO

GOAL MACHINE

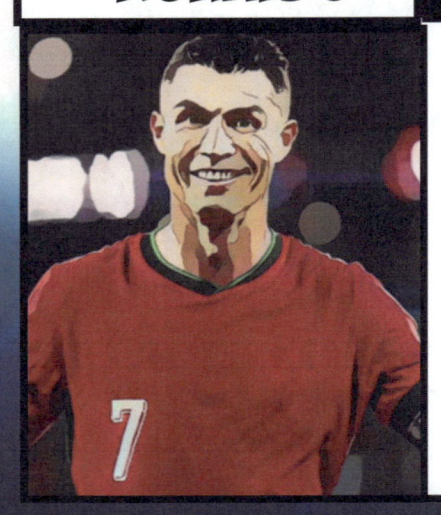

A GOAL MACHINE, WON 5 CHAMPIONS LEAGUES, EURO 2016, 3 PREMIER LEAGUE TITLES WITH MANCHESTER UNITED, 2 LA LIGA TITLES WITH REAL MADRID, 2 SERIE A TITLES WITH JUVENTUS, AND HAS SCORED 923+ CAREER GOALS.

GREATEST WOMEN'S PLAYER EVER

MARTA

6-TIME FIFA BEST PLAYER, 7 SWEDISH LEAGUE TITLES WITH TYRESÖ & ROSENGÅRD, 2 COPA AMÉRICA TITLES, AND BRAZIL'S ALL-TIME TOP SCORER WITH 115 INTERNATIONAL GOALS. SHE HAS SCORED OVER 600 CAREER GOALS ACROSS CLUB AND INTERNATIONAL MATCHES.

PLAYERS

BEST PLAYERS OF ALL TIME

MESSI

THE GOAT

- **GOALS:** 850+ CAREER GOALS
- **ASSISTS:** OVER 350 ASSISTS (MOST IN HISTORY)
- **TROPHIES:** 44 TOTAL TITLES (MOST BY ANY PLAYER!)
- **WORLD CUP:** 🏆 2022
- **COPA AMÉRICA:** 🏆 2021
- **LA LIGA TITLES:** 🏆 10 (BARCELONA)
- **CHAMPIONS LEAGUE TITLES:** 🏆 4 (BARCELONA)
- **BALLON D'ORS:** 🏆 8 (RECORD!)

Lionel Messi is one of the greatest soccer players of all time, known for his magical dribbling, insane goals, and record-breaking achievements.

Messi spent 17 seasons at Barcelona, winning 10 La Liga titles and 4 Champions Leagues, while scoring an unbelievable 672 goals for the club. He later moved to PSG, winning 2 Ligue 1 titles, and now plays in the MLS with Inter Miami.

With Argentina, he's the country's all-time top scorer (106 goals) and led them to Copa América victory in 2021 before finally lifting the World Cup in 2022. Messi has won a record 8 Ballon d'Or awards, more than anyone in history!

IN 2012, MESSI SCORED 91 GOALS IN A SINGLE CALENDAR YEAR!

THAT'S MORE THAN ENTIRE TEAMS SCORED IN THEIR LEAGUES THAT SEASON.

HE OUTSCORED BIG CLUBS LIKE MANCHESTER UNITED, CHELSEA, AND BORUSSIA DORTMUND THAT YEAR!

RIVALRIES

WHAT IS A RIVALRY?

A SOCCER RIVALRY IS WHEN TWO TEAMS HAVE A LONG HISTORY OF COMPETING FIERCELY AGAINST EACH OTHER, MAKING THEIR MATCHES EXTRA EXCITING FOR PLAYERS AND FANS.

LETS LOOK AT THE 3 BIGGEST IN THE WORLD

RIVALRIES

THE BIGGEST SOCCER RIVALRIES IN HISTORY

OUR TEAM IS BETTER!

RIVALRIES

> THE FIRST EVER GAME TOOK PLACE 1913. RIVER PLATE WON 2-1

SUPERCLÁSICO

3RD

BOCA JUNIORS **VS** RIVER PLATE

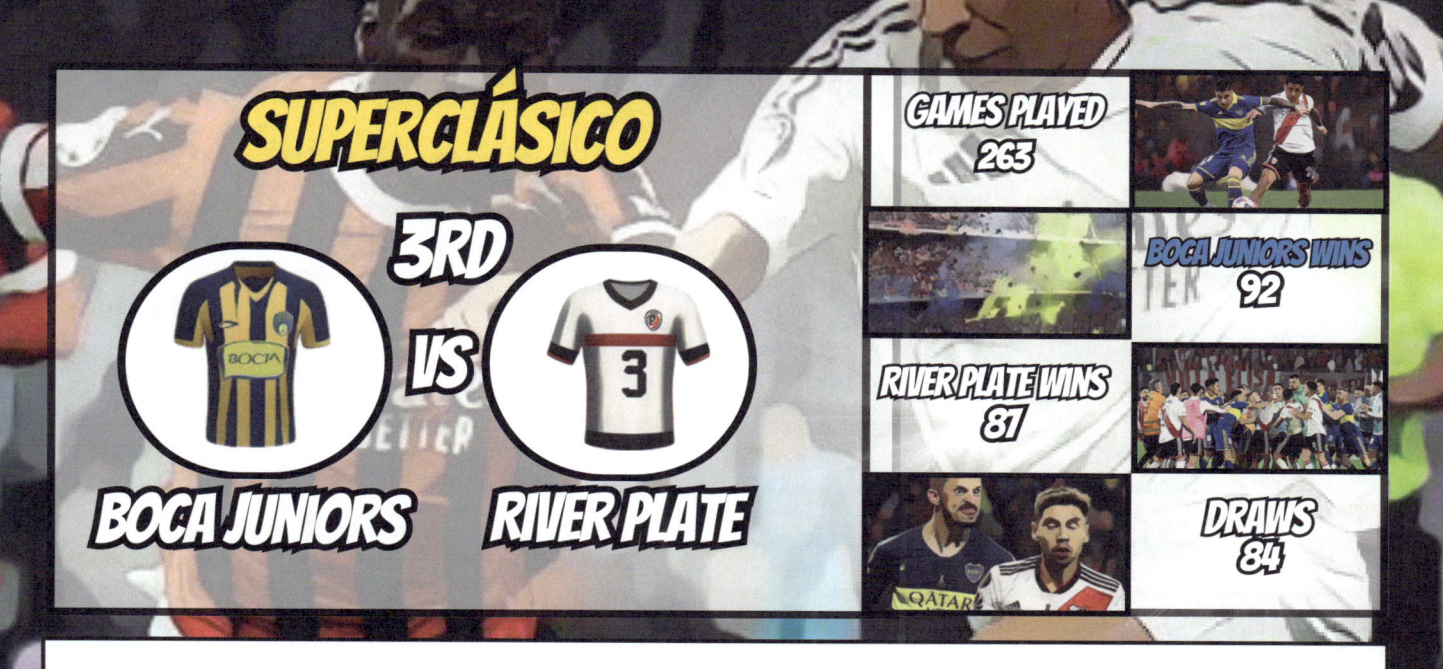

- **GAMES PLAYED** 263
- **BOCA JUNIORS WINS** 92
- **RIVER PLATE WINS** 87
- **DRAWS** 84

IN ARGENTINA, THERE'S NO BIGGER GAME THAN BOCA JUNIORS VS. RIVER PLATE—THE SUPERCLÁSICO! THESE TWO TEAMS STARTED IN LA BOCA, BUT WHEN RIVER MOVED TO A RICHER AREA, THE RIVALRY EXPLODED..

LA BOMBONERA SHAKES! - BOCA'S STADIUM VIBRATES WHEN FANS JUMP, AND IT HAS EVEN BEEN MEASURED ON THE RICHTER SCALE!

WITH FIERY MATCHES, CRAZY GOALS, AND EVEN GAMES STOPPED BY TEAR GAS, THIS IS ONE OF THE WORLD'S MOST INTENSE SOCCER BATTLES. WHETHER IT'S IN LEAGUE GAMES, CUPS, THE SUPERCLÁSICO IS ALWAYS FULL OF DRAMA.

RIVALRIES

OVER 130 YEARS OF BATTLES! THE FIRST OLD FIRM MATCH WAS PLAYED IN 1888.

OLD FIRM

CELTIC 2ND VS **RANGERS**

GAMES PLAYED **444**

CELTIC WINS **170**

RANGERS WINS **170**

DRAWS **104**

THE OLD FIRM RIVALRY BETWEEN CELTIC AND RANGERS, WHICH BEGAN IN 1888, IS ONE OF THE LONGEST-RUNNING TOP-LEVEL RIVALRIES S IN THE WORLD!

CELTIC WAS FOUNDED BY IRISH IMMIGRANTS AND HAS STRONG TIES TO CATHOLIC TRADITIONS, WHILE RANGERS HAS HISTORICALLY REPRESENTED SCOTTISH PROTESTANT COMMUNITIES. OVER THE YEARS, THEIR RIVALRY HAS GROWN BEYOND SPORTS, FUELING SOME OF THE MOST INTENSE AND PASSIONATE GAMES IN THE WORLD.

UNBEATEN SEASONS! BOTH CLUBS HAVE HAD "INVINCIBLE" SEASONS, GOING UNDEFEATED IN THE LEAGUE—RANGERS IN 1899 AND 2021, AND CELTIC IN 2017.

BETWEEN THEM, CELTIC AND RANGERS HAVE WON OVER 120 SCOTTISH LEAGUE TITLES, MEANING THEY'VE DOMINATED SCOTTISH SOCCER FOR MORE THAN A CENTURY.

IN 2011, AN OLD FIRM MATCH HAD 34 FOULS, 13 YELLOW CARDS, 3 RED CARDS, AND EVEN A FIGHT BETWEEN COACHES!

RIVALRIES

REAL MADRID'S BIGGEST VICTORY WAS 11-1 IN 1943, WHILE BARCELONA'S BIGGEST WAS 7-2 IN 1950.

EL CLÁSICO

1ST
BARCELONA VS **REAL MADRID**

GAMES PLAYED 259

BARCELONA 102

REAL MADRID 105

DRAWS 52

El Clásico isn't just a soccer game—it's a battle for pride, history, and bragging rights. These two clubs have been fighting for dominance since 1902, with Barcelona winning the first match 3-1!

But this rivalry runs deeper than soccer. Barcelona represents Catalan pride and independence, while Real Madrid has long been tied to Spanish nationalism.

Over the years, the greatest players in history—Messi, Ronaldo, Maradona, Ronaldinho, Zidane, and more—have all left their mark on this legendary fixture.

El Clásico attracts over 600 million viewers worldwide—that's nearly twice the population of the USA!

The red card king! Sergio Ramos holds the record for the most red cards (5) in El Clásico history—ouch!

RIVALRIES

OTHER FAMOUS RIVALRIES

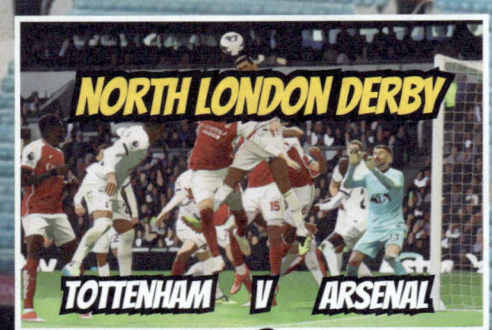

NORTH LONDON DERBY
TOTTENHAM V ARSENAL

WHY? ARSENAL AND TOTTENHAM HAVE BEEN BITTER RIVALS SINCE 1913, WHEN ARSENAL MOVED FROM SOUTH LONDON TO NORTH LONDON, STEPPING INTO SPURS' TERRITORY. THE RIVALRY IS ABOUT MORE THAN JUST GEOGRAPHY—IT'S ABOUT BRAGGING RIGHTS, HISTORY, AND PASSIONATE FANBASES THAT CAN'T STAND EACH OTHER.

MILAN DERBY
AC MILAN VS INTER MILAN

WHY? THE DERBY DELLA MADONNINA IS ONE OF THE FEW RIVALRIES WHERE BOTH TEAMS SHARE THE SAME STADIUM, THE SAN SIRO. AC MILAN WAS TRADITIONALLY THE CLUB OF THE WORKING CLASS, WHILE INTER ATTRACTED THE MORE ELITE AND INTERNATIONAL FANBASE. THEIR CLASHES HAVE SEEN RED CARDS, FLARES THROWN ON THE PITCH, AND UNFORGETTABLE GOALS.

NORTH WEST DERBY
LIVERPOOL VS MAN UTD

WHY? THESE TWO CLUBS ARE ENGLAND'S MOST SUCCESSFUL TEAMS, AND THEIR RIVALRY GOES BACK TO THE INDUSTRIAL COMPETITION BETWEEN THE CITIES OF MANCHESTER AND LIVERPOOL. BOTH CLUBS HAVE DOMINATED DIFFERENT ERAS OF ENGLISH FOOTBALL—LIVERPOOL RULED THE 70S AND 80S, WHILE UNITED DOMINATED THE 90S AND 2000S. THEIR GAMES ARE ALWAYS FIERCE, PHYSICAL, AND PACKED WITH DRAMA.

DER KLASSIKER
DORTMUND VS BAYERN

WHY? BAYERN MUNICH IS THE MOST SUCCESSFUL CLUB IN GERMAN HISTORY, WHILE BORUSSIA DORTMUND IS SEEN AS THE PEOPLE'S CLUB, WITH ONE OF THE MOST PASSIONATE FAN BASES IN EUROPE. THEIR RIVALRY INTENSIFIED IN THE 2010S, WHEN DORTMUND WON BACK-TO-BACK BUNDESLIGA TITLES UNDER JÜRGEN KLOPP, CHALLENGING BAYERN'S DOMINANCE.

"SOME PEOPLE THINK FOOTBALL IS A MATTER OF LIFE AND DEATH. I ASSURE YOU, IT'S MUCH MORE SERIOUS THAN THAT."

— BILL SHANKLY (LEGENDARY LIVERPOOL MANAGER)

RIVALRIES

OLDEST IN HISTORY

SCOTLAND VS ENGLAND

MOST GAMES PLAYED! ENGLAND VS. SCOTLAND IS THE MOST-PLAYED INTERNATIONAL FIXTURE EVER, WITH OVER 115 MATCHES!

BIGGEST WIN EVER! ENGLAND ONCE BEAT SCOTLAND 9-3 IN 1961, THEIR BIGGEST WIN IN THE RIVALRY. SCOTLAND GOT REVENGE IN 1928, WINNING 5-1 AT WEMBLEY—EARNING THE NICKNAME "THE WEMBLEY WIZARDS"!

- ENGLAND AND SCOTLAND ARE RIGHT NEXT TO EACH OTHER, BUT ON THE SOCCER FIELD, THEY'RE FIERCE RIVALS!

- THEIR FIRST MATCH IN 1872 ENDED 0-0, STARTING A BATTLE FOR BRAGGING RIGHTS THAT HAS LASTED OVER 150 YEARS.

- SCOTLAND'S MOST FAMOUS WIN CAME IN 1967, BEATING ENGLAND 3-2, JUST AFTER ENGLAND WON THE WORLD CUP—SCOTTISH FANS EVEN CALLED THEMSELVES THE "UNOFFICIAL WORLD CHAMPIONS"!

CROWD MADNESS! IN 1937, A RECORD 149,415 FANS PACKED HAMPDEN PARK IN SCOTLAND TO WATCH THEM PLAY ENGLAND—THE BIGGEST-EVER CROWD FOR AN INTERNATIONAL MATCH!

COMPETITIONS

THE MOST FAMOUS COMPETITIONS WORLDWIDE

SOCCER IS PLAYED EVERYWHERE, BUT SOME TOURNAMENTS ARE BIGGER, LOUDER, AND MORE EXCITING THAN THE REST! FROM THE WORLD CUP, WHERE NATIONS BATTLE FOR GLORY, TO THE CHAMPIONS LEAGUE, WHERE THE BEST CLUBS IN EUROPE FACE OFF, THESE COMPETITIONS BRING LEGENDARY PLAYERS, UNFORGETTABLE MOMENTS, AND MILLIONS OF FANS TOGETHER. GET READY TO EXPLORE THE MOST FAMOUS SOCCER TOURNAMENTS ON THE PLANET!

INTERNATIONAL

CRISTIANO RONALDO IS THE TOURNAMENT'S ALL-TIME TOP SCORER WITH 140 GOALS—MORE THAN OVER 450 ENTIRE CLUBS THAT HAVE COMPETED IN THE COMPETITION!

CHAMPIONS LEAGUE

STARTED: 1955

TEAMS: 32 (BUT 80 TRY TO QUALIFY)

WHEN: EVERY YEAR

WHERE: EUROPE

BIGGEST WINNER: REAL MADRID (15 TIMES)

DIFFCULTY: ★★★★½

THE UEFA CHAMPIONS LEAGUE IS EUROPE'S BIGGEST CLUB COMPETITION, LAUNCHED IN 1955 AS THE EUROPEAN CUP BEFORE REBRANDING IN 1992. IT BRINGS TOGETHER THE BEST CLUBS FROM ACROSS EUROPE, WITH TOP TEAMS QUALIFYING THROUGH THEIR DOMESTIC LEAGUES.

ORIGINALLY A 16-TEAM KNOCKOUT TOURNAMENT, IT EXPANDED OVER THE YEARS AND NOW FEATURES A GROUP STAGE WITH 32 TEAMS, FOLLOWED BY KNOCKOUT ROUNDS LEADING TO THE FINAL. REAL MADRID IS THE MOST SUCCESSFUL CLUB, WITH 14 TITLES, WHILE LEGENDS LIKE MESSI, RONALDO, ZIDANE, AND MALDINI HAVE MADE HISTORY IN THE COMPETITION.

WITH DRAMATIC COMEBACKS, THRILLING FINALS, AND ICONIC MOMENTS, THE CHAMPIONS LEAGUE IS THE ULTIMATE STAGE FOR CLUB FOOTBALL.

INTERNATIONAL

ALL CHAMPIONS LEAGUE/EUROPEAN CUP WINNERS

REAL MADRID - 🏆 14

AC MILAN - 🏆 7

BAYERN MUNICH - 🏆 6

LIVERPOOL - 🏆 6

BARCELONA - 🏆 5

AJAX - 🏆 4

MANCHESTER UNITED - 🏆 3

INTER MILAN - 🏆 3

JUVENTUS - 🏆 2

BENFICA - 🏆 2

NOTTINGHAM FOREST - 🏆 2

PORTO - 🏆 2

CHELSEA - 🏆 2

MAN CITY - 🏆 1

CELTIC - 🏆 1

HAMBURG - 🏆 1

STEAUA BUCHAREST - 🏆 1

MARSEILLE - 🏆 1

BORUSSIA DORTMUND - 🏆 1

FEYENOORD - 🏆 1

ASTON VILLA - 🏆 1

PSV EINDHOVEN - 🏆 1

RED STAR BELGRADE - 🏆 1

INTERNATIONAL

THE OLDEST INTERNATIONAL SOCCER TOURNAMENT

COPA AMERICA

STARTED: 1916

TEAMS: 16

WHEN: EVERY 4 YEARS

WHERE: NORTH AND SOUTH AMERICA

BIGGEST WINNER: ARGENTINA/URUGUAY (15 EACH)

DIFFCULTY: ★★★★☆

The first edition was held in Argentina to celebrate the country's 100th anniversary of independence, with Argentina, Brazil, Uruguay, and Chile competing. Uruguay won that first tournament, beginning a long tradition of intense South American rivalries.

The tournament features all 10 CONMEBOL nations—Argentina, Bolivia, Brazil, Chile, Colombia, Ecuador, Paraguay, Peru, Uruguay, and Venezuela—with guest teams often invited from North and Central America. Since 1993, Copa América has usually had 12 teams (10 from South America + 2 guests), but special editions like 2016 and 2024 have expanded to 16 teams.

With its fast-paced matches, passionate fans, and legendary players—from Pelé and Maradona to Messi and Neymar—Copa América is one of the most exciting tournaments in world football, showcasing the best of South American talent.

INTERNATIONAL

> THE FIRST-EVER FINAL IN 1960 HAD ONLY 17,966 FANS IN THE STADIUM, WHILE THE 2021 FINAL AT WEMBLEY HAD OVER 67,000

EURO CUP

STARTED : 1960

TEAMS : 24

WHEN : EVERY 4 YEARS

WHERE : EUROPE

BIGGEST WINNER : SPAIN (4 TIMES)

DIFFCULTY : ★★★★★

The UEFA European Championship (Euro Cup) kicked off in 1960, thanks to a Frenchman named Henri Delaunay, who had the idea way back in the 1920s! But it wasn't until after his passing that the first tournament finally happened, with just four teams battling for the trophy. The Soviet Union won the first-ever Euros by beating Yugoslavia 2-1.

Over time, the tournament grew—expanding to 8 teams in 1980, then 16 in 1996, and now 24 teams compete for the crown!

With thrilling matches, roaring fans, and legendary players, the Euros are one of the biggest tournaments in world football

DID YOU KNOW?

In 2004, Greece pulled off one of the biggest upsets in soccer history by winning the Euro Cup! They had never won a major tournament before and were huge underdogs, but with strong defense, smart tactics, and a never-give-up attitude,

They shocked everyone. They defeated host nation Portugal twice, including a 1-0 win in the final, proving that even the biggest dreams can come true!

INTERNATIONAL

WORLD CUP

OVER 3 BILLION PEOPLE WATCH!

STARTED: 1930

TEAMS: 48

WHEN: EVERY 4 YEARS

WHERE: WORLDWIDE

BIGGEST WINNER: BRAZIL (5 TIMES)

DIFFCULTY: ★★★★★

THE FIFA WORLD CUP KICKED OFF IN 1930, WHEN FOOTBALL'S BIGGEST TOURNAMENT WAS BORN! THE IDEA CAME FROM JULES RIMET, A FRENCHMAN WHO WANTED A GLOBAL COMPETITION WHERE NATIONS COULD BATTLE FOR SOCCER GLORY. THE FIRST-EVER WORLD CUP WAS HELD IN URUGUAY, WITH ONLY 13 TEAMS—AND THE HOSTS URUGUAY WON, DEFEATING ARGENTINA 4-2 IN THE FINAL.

AT FIRST, ONLY A FEW TEAMS FROM EUROPE AND SOUTH AMERICA PARTICIPATED, AS TRAVELING ACROSS THE WORLD WAS EXPENSIVE. IN 1958, THE TOURNAMENT TRULY BECAME GLOBAL WHEN PELE, JUST 17 YEARS OLD, HELPED BRAZIL WIN THEIR FIRST-EVER TITLE—BECOMING THE YOUNGEST PLAYER TO SCORE IN A WORLD CUP FINAL!

TODAY, 32 TEAMS COMPETE FOR THE FAMOUS GOLDEN TROPHY, MAKING THE WORLD CUP THE MOST-WATCHED SPORTING EVENT ON THE PLANET!

INTERNATIONAL

THE MOST SUCCESSFUL WORLD CUP WINNERS

BRAZIL - 🏆 5 (1958, 1962, 1970, 1994, 2002)

GERMANY - 🏆 4 (1954, 1974, 1990*, 2014)

ITALY - 🏆 4 (1934, 1938, 1982, 2006)

ARGENTINA - 🏆 3 (1978, 1986, 2022)

URUGUAY - 🏆 2 (1930, 1950)

FRANCE - 🏆 2 (1998, 2018)

ENGLAND - 🏆 1 (1966)

SPAIN - 🏆 1 (2010)

OLDEST

THE OLDEST NATIONAL FOOTBALL COMPETITION IN THE WORLD

THE FA CUP 🏴󠁧󠁢󠁥󠁮󠁧󠁿

The FA Cup, founded in 1871, is the oldest soccer competition in the world and one of the most exciting! What makes it special? Any team in England—from tiny amateur clubs to the biggest Premier League giants—can enter. That means underdogs sometimes beat the biggest teams, creating legendary "giant-killing" moments.

The tournament starts with hundreds of teams battling in early rounds, leading up to the final at Wembley Stadium, where the winners lift the famous FA Cup trophy

- In 2012, non-league team Basingstoke Town had no stadium, so they played their FA Cup "home" game at their opponent's ground—and still won!

- In 1971, Alvechurch and Oxford City played six matches (660 minutes total) to settle their FA Cup tie before penalties even existed!

- In 1887, Preston North End destroyed Hyde 26-0, the biggest scoreline in FA Cup history!

- Arsenal holds the record for the most FA Cup victories, having won the prestigious tournament 14 times.

DID YOU KNOW?

IN 1895, ASTON VILLA WON THE FA CUP, ENGLAND'S BIGGEST SOCCER TROPHY. BUT AFTER THEIR VICTORY, SOMETHING SHOCKING HAPPENED—THE CUP WAS STOLEN!

SOMEONE TOOK IT FROM A SHOP WINDOW WHERE IT WAS ON DISPLAY, AND FOR YEARS, NOBODY KNEW WHERE IT WAS.

THEN, IN 1899, A DOG NAMED PICKLES BECAME A HERO! WHILE SNIFFING AROUND IN A GARDEN, PICKLES FOUND SOMETHING BURIED UNDER A BUSH— IT WAS THE MISSING FA CUP! HIS OWNER BECAME FAMOUS, AND PICKLES BECAME A NATIONAL HERO, EVEN GETTING FREE FOOD FOR LIFE AS A REWARD!

TO THIS DAY, PICKLES IS REMEMBERED AS THE DOG WHO SAVED ENGLISH SOCCER HISTORY!

DOMESTIC

THE TOP 5 DOMESTIC CLUB LEAGUES ACROSS THE WORLD

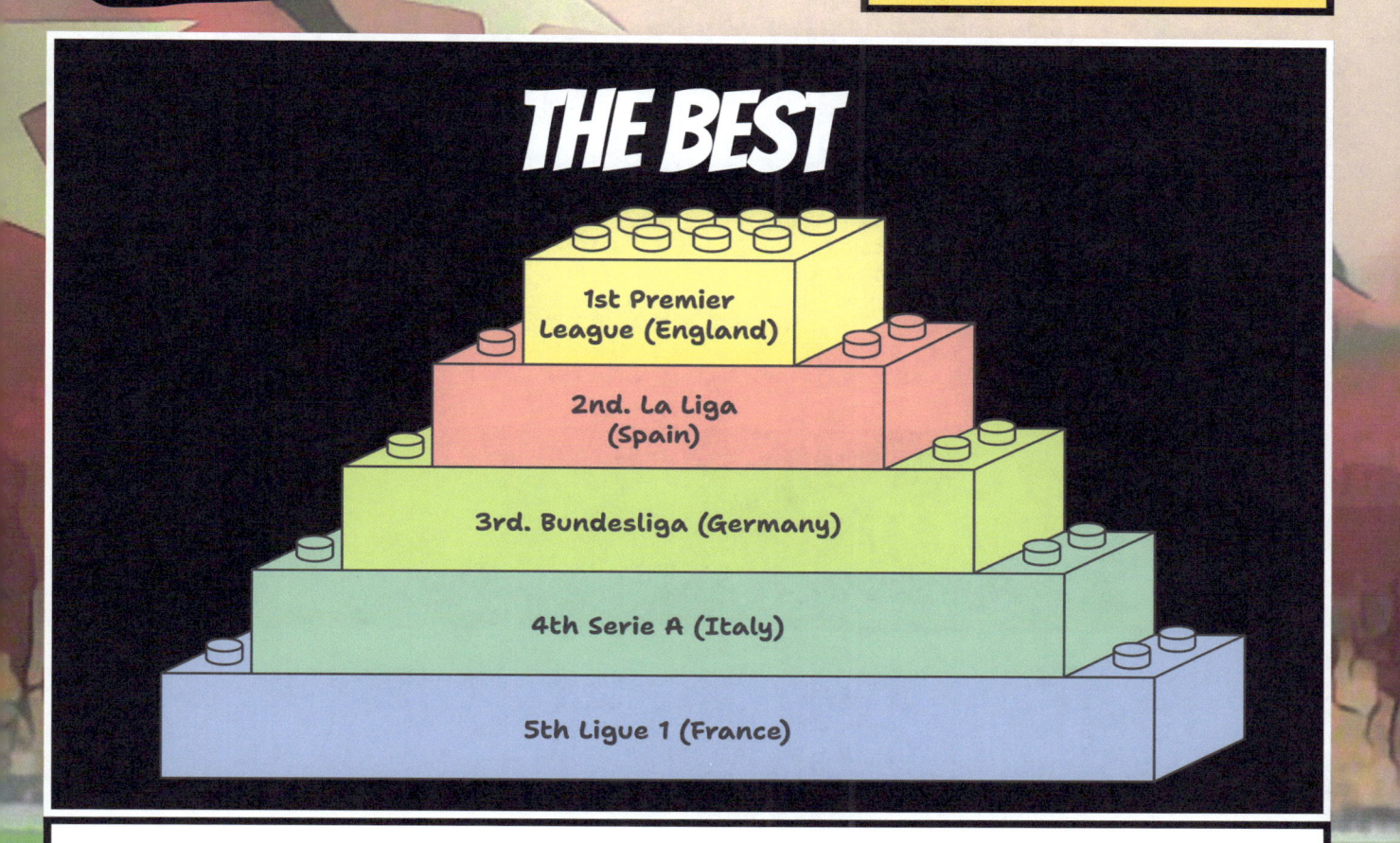

THE BEST

- 1st Premier League (England)
- 2nd. La Liga (Spain)
- 3rd. Bundesliga (Germany)
- 4th Serie A (Italy)
- 5th Ligue 1 (France)

A domestic league is like a big soccer season where teams from the same country play against each other to see who's the best! Every team plays home and away matches, trying to earn the most points to win the league title.

The best teams qualify for big international tournaments, while the worst teams might get relegated (moved down to a lower division). Each country has its own league, like the Premier League in England or La Liga in Spain, making every season full of goals, drama, and exciting rivalries!

DOMESTIC

THE TOP 5 LEAGUES ACROSS THE WORLD

PREMIER LEAGUE ★★★★★

STARTED IN 1888 BUT RENAMED IN 1992, THE PREMIER LEAGUE IS THE FASTEST, MOST-WATCHED LEAGUE ON THE PLANET. TEAMS LIKE MANCHESTER UNITED, LIVERPOOL, AND MANCHESTER CITY BATTLE IN FRONT OF PACKED STADIUMS AND MILLIONS OF FANS WORLDWIDE. IT'S FAMOUS FOR ITS NON-STOP ACTION, UNPREDICTABLE RESULTS, AND LEGENDARY PLAYERS LIKE CRISTIANO RONALDO AND THIERRY HENRY.

LA LIGA ★★★★½

FOUNDED IN 1929, LA LIGA IS HOME TO BARCELONA AND REAL MADRID, TWO OF THE BIGGEST CLUBS IN HISTORY. IT'S KNOWN FOR ITS BEAUTIFUL PASSING PLAY, TIKI-TAKA STYLE, AND GOAT DEBATES BETWEEN MESSI AND RONALDO. THE WORLD HAS WITNESSED UNFORGETTABLE MOMENTS FROM LEGENDS LIKE PELÉ, MARADONA, AND ZIDANE IN SPAIN'S TOP LEAGUE.

SERIE A ★★★★☆

ONE OF THE OLDEST LEAGUES, SERIE A BEGAN IN 1898 AND IS FAMOUS FOR ITS TACTICAL BATTLES, STRONG DEFENSES, AND WORLD-CLASS STRIKERS. CLUBS LIKE AC MILAN, JUVENTUS, AND INTER MILAN HAVE DOMINATED EUROPEAN SOCCER, AND STARS LIKE DIEGO MARADONA, FRANCESCO TOTTI, AND ZLATAN IBRAHIMOVIĆ BECAME LEGENDS HERE.

DID YOU KNOW?

IN 2016, LEICESTER CITY PULLED OFF THE GREATEST SHOCK IN SOCCER HISTORY, WINNING THE PREMIER LEAGUE AFTER STARTING THE SEASON AS **5,000-TO-1** UNDERDOGS!

A TEAM THAT BARELY AVOIDED RELEGATION THE YEAR BEFORE STUNNED THE WORLD, BEATING GIANTS LIKE MANCHESTER UNITED AND CHELSEA.

LED BY JAMIE VARDY'S GOALS, N'GOLO KANTÉ'S ENERGY, AND RIYAD MAHREZ'S MAGIC, LEICESTER'S FAIRYTALE RUN PROVED THAT ANYTHING IS POSSIBLE IN SOCCER!

DOMESTIC

THE TOP 5 LEAGUES ACROSS THE WORLD

BUNDESLIGA ★★★★☆

Founded in 1963, the Bundesliga is known for high-energy matches, passionate fans, and incredible goal-scoring. Bayern Munich is the powerhouse, winning most titles but teams like Borussia Dortmund and RB Leipzig keep things exciting. With the world's highest average attendance, German soccer is pure electric!

LIGUE 1 ★★★☆☆

The French league started in 1932, but in recent years, Paris Saint-Germain (PSG) has dominated with superstars like Lionel Messi, Neymar, and Kylian Mbappé. Known for developing young talent, Ligue 1 has produced icons like Zidane and Thierry Henry, making it a hotbed for future legends.

OTHER LEAGUES

SPFL · MLS · LIGA · SüperLig · BRASILEIRÃO · Jupiler Pro League

GAMES

THE MOST LEGENDARY GAMES OF ALL TIME

SOCCER IS FULL OF MAGIC—ONE MOMENT, A TEAM LOOKS BEATEN, AND THE NEXT, THEY'RE CELEBRATING AN IMPOSSIBLE COMEBACK!

SOME GAMES ARE SO DRAMATIC, SO SHOCKING, AND SO THRILLING THAT FANS REMEMBER THEM FOREVER. FROM LAST-MINUTE WINNERS TO UNDERDOG VICTORIES,

THESE ARE SOME OF THE GREATEST MATCHES IN SOCCER HISTORY!

EPIC GAMES

NUMBER 5

1950 WORLD CUP FINAL
URUGUAY 2 VS. 1 BRAZIL

Brazil was so sure they would win that they had a victory parade planned before the match! But Uruguay stunned 200,000 Brazilian fans in Rio's Maracanã Stadium, coming from behind to win 2-1. The moment was so heartbreaking for Brazil that it was called the "Maracanazo"—one of the most shocking upsets ever.

EPIC GAMES

NUMBER 4

BRAZIL'S WORST NIGHTMARE
2014 WORLD CUP SEMIFINAL
GERMANY 7 VS 1 BRAZIL.

This was supposed to be Brazil's big moment, playing the World Cup at home. Instead, Germany crushed them in a crazy 7-1 defeat, scoring five goals in the first half-hour! Brazilian fans cried in the stands, and the match became one of the biggest humiliations in soccer history.

EPIC GAMES

NUMBER 3

THE ULTIMATE LAST-MINUTE COMEBACK
1999 CHAMPIONS LEAGUE FINAL
MANCHESTER UNITED 2 VS 1 BAYERN MUNICH

Bayern Munich was just seconds away from lifting the Champions League trophy, leading 1-0 in stoppage time. But Manchester United pulled off a miracle, scoring two goals in three minutes to steal the victory! The Bayern players were in tears as United celebrated an unbelievable comeback.

DID YOU KNOW?

BORUSSIA DORTMUND HAS THE BIGGEST STANDING TERRACE IN ALL OF EUROPE, CALLED DIE GELBE WAND (THE YELLOW WALL).

OVER 25,00 FANS IN JUST ONE STAND!

EPIC GAMES

NUMBER 2

THE HAND OF GOD & GOAL OF THE CENTURY
1986 WORLD CUP QUARTERFINAL
ARGENTINA 2 VS 1 ENGLAND

In one match, Diego Maradona became a legend! First, he cheekily punched the ball into the net (and got away with it!), calling it the "Hand of God."

Minutes later, he dribbled past five England players to score the "Goal of the Century," proving he was simply unstoppable.

EPIC GAMES

NUMBER 1

THE MIRACLE OF ISTANBUL
2005 CHAMPIONS LEAGUE FINAL
LIVERPOOL 3 VS 3 AC MILAN
(LIVERPOOL WON ON PENALTIES)

At halftime, Liverpool was losing 3-0 and looked completely beaten. But in just six crazy minutes, they scored three goals to tie the game!

After a tense extra time, goalkeeper Jerzy Dudek became the hero in the penalty shootout, helping Liverpool complete one of the greatest comebacks ever! Winning the Champions League

RECORDS

CRAZY SOCCER RECORDS FROM AROUND THE WORLD

THAT'S CRAZY !!!

86

CRAZY RECORDS

CRAZY SOCCER RECORDS

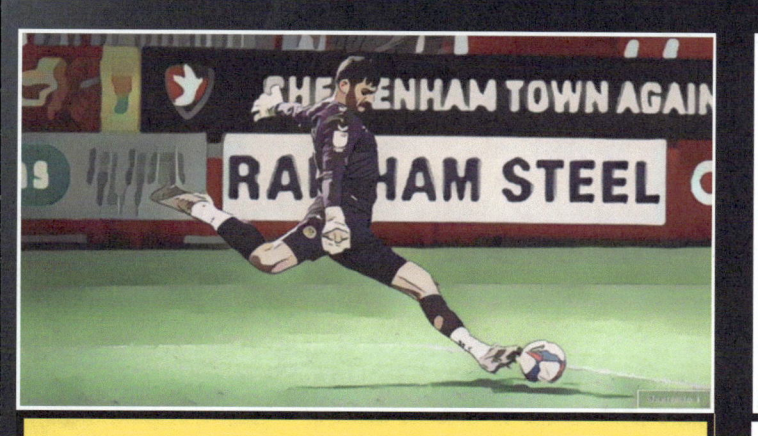

LONGEST GOAL EVER

TOM KING (105 YARDS!)

IN 2021, GOALKEEPER TOM KING SCORED A GOAL FROM HIS OWN PENALTY BOX! HIS MASSIVE KICK FLEW 105 YARDS (96 METERS), BOUNCED OVER THE OTHER GOALIE'S HEAD, AND INTO THE NET. THAT'S ALMOST THE ENTIRE LENGTH OF A SOCCER FIELD!

CRAZIEST SCORELINE

149-0!

YES, YOU READ THAT RIGHT! IN 2002, A MADAGASCAR TEAM SCORED 149 GOALS IN ONE MATCH—BUT NOT HOW YOU THINK. ANGRY ABOUT A REFEREE DECISION, THEY SCORED EVERY GOAL INTO THEIR OWN NET AS A PROTEST. DEFINITELY NOT THE BEST WAY TO WIN A GAME!

CRAZY RECORDS

CRAZY SOCCER RECORDS

MOST GOALS IN A SINGLE GAME

16!

Argentine legend Stephan Stanis holds the record for most goals scored by one player in a match,

Netting 16 goals in a single game in 1942. That's more goals than some players score in their entire careers!

FASTEST GOAL EVER

2.1 SECONDS!

In 2009, Nawaf Al-Abed scored straight from kick-off in just 2.1 seconds!

Before the other team even blinked, the ball was in the net. Now that's what you call starting fast!

CRAZY RECORDS

CRAZY SOCCER RECORDS

MOST RED CARDS IN A SINGLE GAME

36!

IN A WILD MATCH IN ARGENTINA, CLAYPOLE VS. VICTORIANO ARENAS (2011) SAW AN UNBELIEVABLE 36 RED CARDS HANDED OUT.

THE GAME DESCENDED INTO CHAOS, WITH THE REFEREE EVENTUALLY SENDING OFF NEARLY EVERYONE.

BY THE END, THERE WERE BARELY ANY PLAYERS LEFT ON THE FIELD!

MOST OWN GOALS IN A GAME

3!

IN 1995, BELGIAN DEFENDER STAN VAN DEN BUYS HAD A NIGHTMARE GAME,

SCORING THREE OWN GOALS IN A SINGLE MATCH. HIS TEAM LOST 3-2, MEANING

HE SINGLE-HANDEDLY GAVE THE OTHER TEAM THE WIN

CRAZY RECORDS

CRAZY SOCCER RECORDS

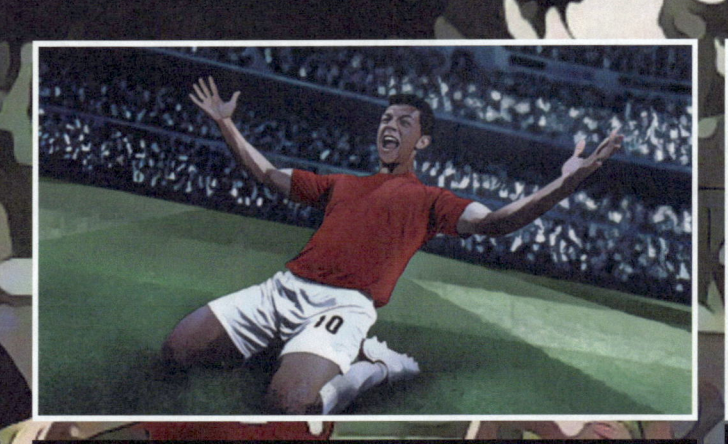

FASTEST HAT-TRICK EVER

90 SECONDS!

IN 1964, TOMMY ROSS FROM SCOTLAND SET AN INCREDIBLE RECORD BY SCORING A HAT-TRICK IN JUST 90 SECONDS!

THAT'S ONE GOAL EVERY 30 SECONDS, A FEAT SO FAST IT'S ALMOST UNBELIEVABLE!

MOST PENALTY SAVES IN A GAME

5!

IN 2016, ITALIAN GOALKEEPER STEFANO SORRENTINO PULLED OFF AN INCREDIBLE FEAT BY SAVING FIVE PENALTIES IN A SINGLE MATCH!

HIS PERFORMANCE WAS SO UNREAL, IT WAS LIKE WATCHING A SUPERHERO IN GOAL!

QUIZ

TEST YOUR SOCCER KNOWLEDGE

QUESTION TIME

QUIZ

TEST YOUR SOCCER KNOWLEDGE

1. WHAT IS THE OLDEST SOCCER COMPETITION IN THE WORLD?

2. WHICH COUNTRY HOSTED THE FIRST-EVER WORLD CUP IN 1930?

3. WHAT IS THE ONLY STADIUM TO HAVE HOSTED TWO WORLD CUP FINALS?

4. HOW MANY PLAYERS ARE ON A SOCCER TEAM DURING A MATCH?

5. WHICH STADIUM HAS THE HIGHEST SEATING CAPACITY IN EUROPE?

6. WHICH STADIUM IS KNOWN AS "THE THEATRE OF DREAMS"?

7. WHERE IS HENNINGSVÆR STADION, THE STUNNING SOCCER FIELD SURROUNDED BY THE SEA?

8. HOW MANY BUSES COULD FIT INSIDE A STANDARD SOCCER FIELD?

9. WHICH CLUB HAS WON THE MOST UEFA CHAMPIONS LEAGUE TITLES?

10. WHICH TWO CLUBS COMPETE IN EL CLÁSICO?

11. WHAT IS THE MOST SUCCESSFUL CLUB IN ITALY BASED ON LEAGUE TITLES?

QUIZ

TEST YOUR SOCCER KNOWLEDGE

12. What is the nickname of Liverpool FC's stadium, Anfield?'

13. What is the famous name for the rivalry between Celtic and Rangers?

14. In which World Cup match did Diego Maradona score both the "Hand of God" goal and the Goal of the Century?

15. What is the biggest club rivalry in Argentina, known for its intense atmosphere?

16. Which two clubs share the San Siro stadium in Italy?

17. Who holds the record for the most goals scored in El Clásico history?

18. In what year did Lionel Messi finally win the FIFA World Cup with Argentina?

19. Which club did Cristiano Ronaldo play for before joining Real Madrid?

20. In the 2018 Copa Libertadores final, where was the second leg played after fan violence forced it to be moved?

BONUS CHALLENGE!
Which player has won the most FIFA Ballon d'Or awards?

QUIZ

ANSWERS

1. THE FA CUP
2. URUGUAY
3. ESTADIO AZTECA (MEXICO, 1970 & 1986)
4. 11 PLAYERS PER TEAM
5. CAMP NOU (BARCELONA, SPAIN - 99,354)
6. OLD TRAFFORD
7. NORWAY (LOFOTEN ISLANDS)
8. ABOUT 238 BUSES
9. REAL MADRID (15 TITLES AS OF 2024)
10. REAL MADRID & BARCELONA
11. JUVENTUS
12. "THE KOP"
13. THE OLD FIRM DERBY
14. 1986 WORLD CUP QUARTER-FINAL (ARGENTINA VS. ENGLAND)
15. SUPERCLÁSICO (BOCA JUNIORS VS. RIVER PLATE)
16. AC MILAN & INTER MILAN
17. LIONEL MESSI (26 GOALS)
18. 2022
19. MANCHESTER UNITED
20. MADRID, SPAIN (SANTIAGO BERNABÉU STADIUM)

BONUS QUESTION = MESSI!

HOW MANY DID YOU GET RIGHT?

THANKS

THANK YOU SO MUCH FOR READING.

LOVE SOCCER? JOIN OUR TEAM!

SCAN THE CODE TO SIGN UP FOR OUR FREE NEWSLETTER AND GET A FREE PRINTABLE (PDF) SOCCER COLORING BOOK

PLUS YOU WILL BE THE FIRST TO GAIN EXCLUSIVE EARLY ACCESS TO MORE SOCCER STORIES, ACTIVITY BOOKS, AND EVEN MORE FREE GIFTS COMING YOUR WAY SOON.

DON'T MISS OUT!

LIKE SOCCER STORIES. CHECK OUT JACK'S SOCCER ADVENTURE AS HE TRADES TEXAS FOR LONDON, IN HIS JOURNEY TO BECOME A STAR! SCAN THE CODE BELOW!

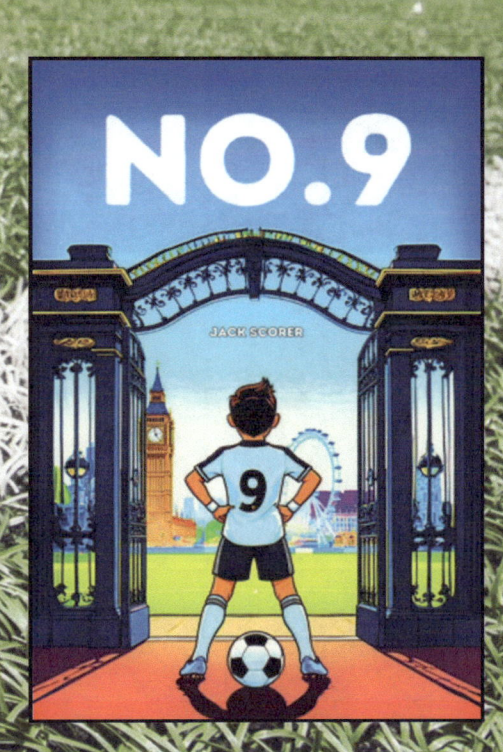

95

Made in United States
Troutdale, OR
03/10/2025